BLESSED NAMES

WHY WAS HE NAMED AL-KADHIM (A)?

WRITTEN BY:
KISA KIDS PUBLICATIONS

Please recite a Fātiḥah for the marḥūmīn
of the Rangwala family, the sponsors of this book.

All proceeds from the sale of this book
will be used to produce more educational resources.

Dedication

This book is dedicated to the beloved Imām of our time (AJ). May Allāh (swt) hasten his reappearance and help us become his true companions.

Acknowledgements

Prophet Muḥammad (s): The pen of a writer is mightier than the blood of a martyr.

True reward lies with Allāh, but we would like to sincerely thank Shaykh Salim Yusufali and Sisters Sabika Mitha Liliana Villalvazo, Zahra Sabur, Kisae Nazar, Sarah Assaf, Nadia Dossani, Fatima Hussain, Naseem Rangwala, a Zehra Abbas. We would especially like to thank Nainava Publications for their contributions. May Allāh bless them this world and the next.

Preface

Prophet Muḥammad (s): Nurture and raise your children in the best way. Raise them with the love of the Prophe and the Ahl al-Bayt (a).

Literature is an influential form of media that often shapes the thoughts and views of an entire generation. Therefor in order to establish an Islamic foundation for the future generations, there is a dire need for compelling Islam literature. Over the past several years, this need has become increasingly prevalent throughout Islamic centers a schools everywhere. Due to the growing dissonance between parents, children, society, and the teachings of Islā and the Ahl al-Bayt (a), this need has become even more pressing. Al-Kisa Foundation, along with its subsidiary, Ki Kids Publications, was conceived in an effort to help bridge this gap with the guidance of ʿulamah and the help educators. We would like to make this a communal effort and platform. Therefore, we sincerely welcome constructi feedback and help in any capacity.

The goal of the *Blessed Names* series is to help children form a lasting bond with the 14 Māʾṣūmīn by learni about and connecting with their names. We hope that you and your children enjoy these books and use them as means to achieve this goal, inshāʾAllāh. We pray to Allāh to give us the strength and tawfīq to perform our duties a responsibilities.

With Duʾās,
Nabi R. Mir (Abidi)

Disclaimer: Religious texts have not been translated verbatim so as to meet the developmental and comprehensi needs of children.
Copyright © 2017; 2019 by Al-Kisa Foundation; SABA Global

All rights reserved. First edition 2017. Second edition 2019. No part of this publication may be reproduced, distributed, or transmitted in any form or by any means, including photocopying, recording, or other electronic or mechanical methods, without the prior written permission of the publisher, except in the case of brief quotations embodied in critical reviews and certain other noncommercial uses permitted by copyright law. For permission requests, please write to the publisher at the address below.

Kisa Kids Publications
4415 Fortran Court
San Jose, CA 95134
(260) KISA-KID [547-2543]

An Introduction to the Blessed Names

Our names are a very special part of us. Many times, they shape our personalities and even explain who we are or the person we would like to become. In this series, you will explore the names and titles of our beloved 14 Ma'soomeen. Did you know that their names and titles were not just ordinary names? They were special because they were given to them by Allah!

Allah has given seven special heavenly names to our Ma'soomeen: Muhammad, Ali, Fatimah, Hasan, Husain, Ja'far, and Musa. Behind each of these names is a heavenly power!

In addition to their names, each of the Ma'soomeen also had special titles by which they became famous. Their titles were often given to them because of the circumstances of their time, but these titles and characteristics were common amongst all the Ma'soomeen. For example, Imam al-Baqir (a) was known for spreading knowledge because he was able to create many new universities and branches of knowledge during his time. However, if the other Ma'soomeen had the same opportunity, they, too, would have spread knowledge and created universities in their teaching circles. In these stories, you will discover some of the reasons why the Ma'soomeen received their specific names or titles.

Many of us share our names with these beloved Ma'soomeen or know people who do. Let's learn about these blessed names and titles so we can strive to be like our blessed Ma'soomeen!

I think al-Kadhim means...

_____

The burning sun shone down brightly on the fields where a drought had plagued the land. A farmer stood in the heat, sweating as he dug into his land with a shovel, preparing for the planting season. From afar, he could see Imam Musa al-Kadhim (a) riding by with his companions on their way to the masjid.

As the Imam (a) grew closer, the farmer scowled and began shouting curses at him. You see, this angry farmer was a friend of the evil caliph of the time, a well-known enemy of the Imam (a), and had heard many lies about the Imam (a). As the farmer drove his shovel into the dirt, he continued to call out names and make fun of the Imam (a), who was now very close to him.

Upon hearing the insults, one of the Imam's companions became very angry with the farmer. He said to the Imam (a), "O Imam (a), this man is disrespecting you! Please let me teach him some manners!" The companion pulled out his sword, ready to fight the farmer.

The other companion chimed in, "Yes, please let us teach this scoundrel a lesson! He cannot talk to our beloved Imam (a) like this!"

Imam al-Kadhim (a) gently raised his hand and everyone instantly became silent. In a calm and gentle voice, he said, "Why don't you two go ahead to the masjid and I'll join you soon, inshaAllah." The companions agreed and bid him farewell.

Imam al-Kadhim (a) then rode toward the angry farmer and said, "Salaamun Alaikum, brother, how are you?"

The farmer scowled and replied bitterly, "I would be better if it weren't for this drought. I've lost everything, and all I have are debts to pay."

With a warm smile, the Imam (a) continued, "Yes, it's been a hard year for many. May Allah give you lots of success in your farming this year. If you don't mind me asking, how much did you lose because of the drought?"

The farmer sighed and said in frustration, "A hundred gold coins!"

Without blinking, the Imam (a) came down from his horse. He reached into his pocket, pulled out a heavy coin bag, and handed it to the farmer. When the farmer opened the bag, he was shocked to see three hundred gold coins inside!

Imam al-Kadhim (a) said with compassion, "This is for you, dear brother. You can pay off your debts, keep your farm, and provide for your family. I pray that Allah sends rain so that your crops flourish this year, inshaAllah!"

The farmer's eyes widened with surprise and his mouth fell open in shock. Embarrassed, he fell to his knees, dropping the bag of coins. With tears in his eyes, he began kissing the Imam's hands and feet, and pleaded, "O my Imam (a)! I am so sorry for my horrible behavior! Everything they said about you is wrong! How could I have been so disrespectful toward you?!"

Imam al-Kadhim (a) helped the farmer off his knees and gently put his arm around him. With a kind voice and smiling face, he forgave him. He then told the farmer, "May Allah be with you," and rode off toward the masjid. The farmer was filled with regret and sadness as he watched the Imam (a) ride away.

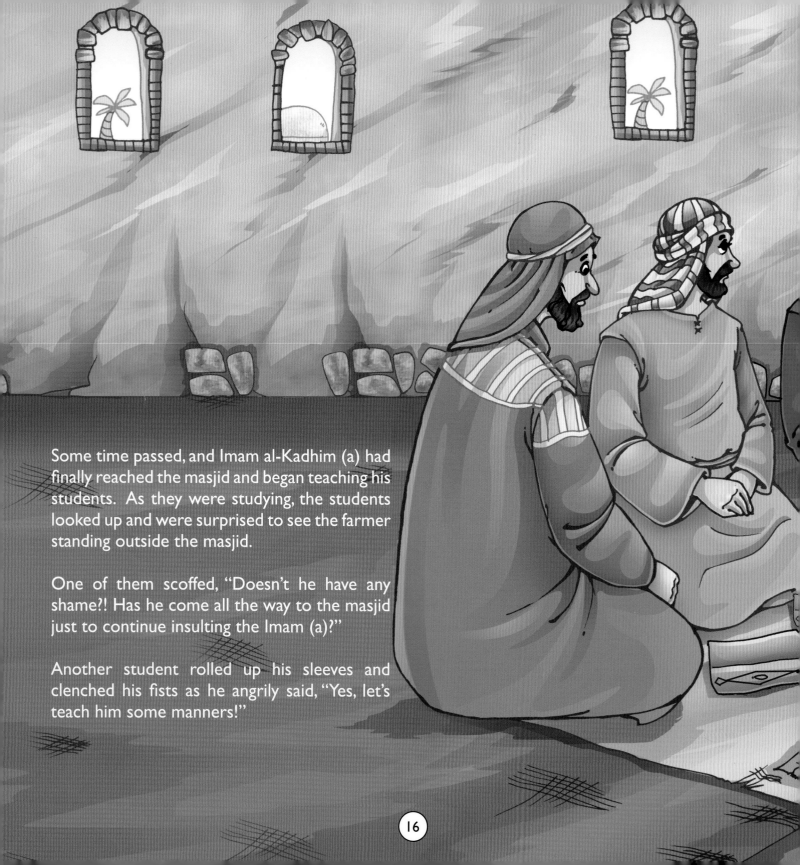

Some time passed, and Imam al-Kadhim (a) had finally reached the masjid and began teaching his students. As they were studying, the students looked up and were surprised to see the farmer standing outside the masjid.

One of them scoffed, "Doesn't he have any shame?! Has he come all the way to the masjid just to continue insulting the Imam (a)?"

Another student rolled up his sleeves and clenched his fists as he angrily said, "Yes, let's teach him some manners!"

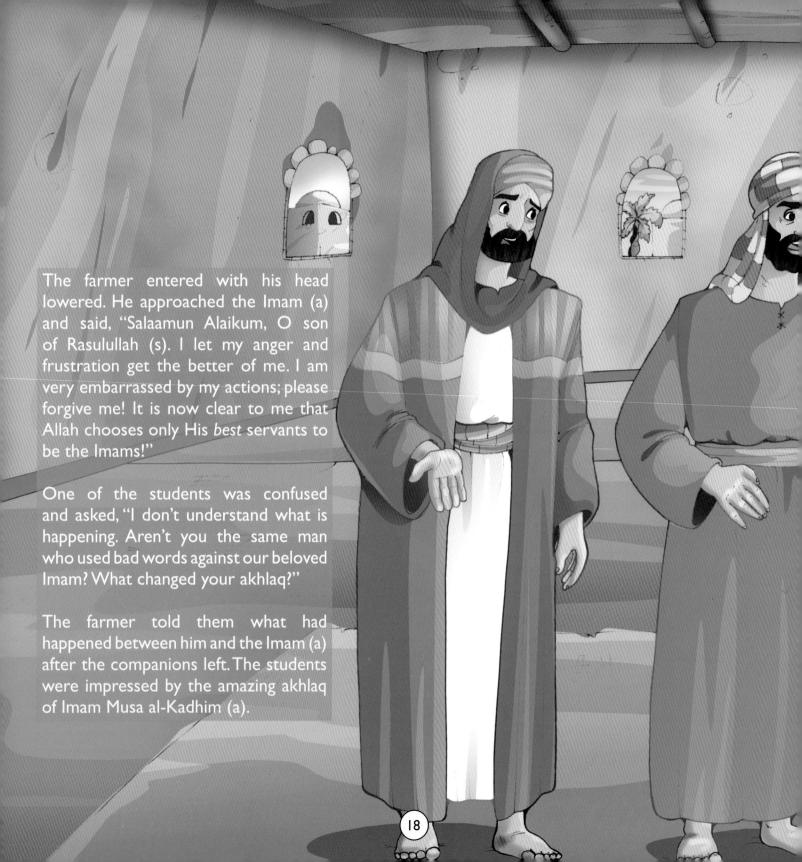

The farmer entered with his head lowered. He approached the Imam (a) and said, "Salaamun Alaikum, O son of Rasulullah (s). I let my anger and frustration get the better of me. I am very embarrassed by my actions; please forgive me! It is now clear to me that Allah chooses only His *best* servants to be the Imams!"

One of the students was confused and asked, "I don't understand what is happening. Aren't you the same man who used bad words against our beloved Imam? What changed your akhlaq?"

The farmer told them what had happened between him and the Imam (a) after the companions left. The students were impressed by the amazing akhlaq of Imam Musa al-Kadhim (a).

18